How-to HR... Get the right staff

Table of Contents

Introduction

Your staff are likely to be the biggest asset to your business but also the biggest cost to your business, not only in terms of wages, but also through employee benefits and employee rights. It is a massive commitment to employ someone – their needs will come before yours. Employment legislation can be a very difficult web to navigate through. Therefore, it is imperative to your business that you hire the right people, comply with current legislation and ultimately get the best from your staff.

After putting all your time and efforts to get your business to where it is today, now that you are ready to take on employees, you want them to be as committed to building the business as you are. You need them to give the best first impression of your business and help work towards your business' goal and objectives. So if you have employees already, ask yourself *'what are your staff currently doing for your business?'* Are they giving the right first impression to customers? Do they offer a helpful and friendly service? Are you allowing them to work to the best of their ability?

I know when I started employing staff in my own business, it was very difficult to let go of the reins and pass some responsibility on to others. This is because I had worked really hard to build reputable business and my reputation and repeat custom now depended on someone else to do a good job on my behalf. But can employees really have the same passion about a business as the owner? I believe that the right staff, with the right training and support can in fact have a great sense of passion about being part of a growing business. A recent study has shown that one of the top motivating factors for employees is a sense of doing a good job! *People Management Magazine, 21 October 2013.*

Throughout this book we will be looking at how to ensure you are in the right position to select the right people to work for you.   Even if you already have employees I strongly recommend that you revisit the beginning of the process and take all things into consideration before hiring any new members of staff.

Recruiting the Right Staff

So, you think you need to hire a new member of staff. It may be your first employee, or not. But how do know who you need? Is it a new appointment or are you replacing someone who has left? It is worth spending time to think about why you need someone else in your business.

Let's look at some reasons for taking on a new employee.

- You need new skills in the business
- To help grow the business or offer new services
- To fill a skills gap which you have identified, i.e. marketing, sales or IT

Some questions you may want to consider: Is this to be a permanent position or maybe to cover a large project? Can you use an agency or external consultant?

Have you identified a problem area within the business? It may be a waste of money if you are recruiting to make up for others' poor performance or lack of qualifications or skills. It would be far cheaper and more rewarding to consider staff training and development. If you take on someone else to smooth over the cracks, they will eventually show through again, bigger than ever!

The two main reasons for recruitment are:

- Creating a new role to grow and expand your business
- Replacing someone who is leaving your business

Creating a new role to grow your business

This is a very exciting time. Maybe your business is outgrowing capacity and you need to add to your team, or you want to develop your business further and need someone with a different skills set to allow this to happen.

Whatever the reasons, you must be clear on what the new employee will be doing. There is no point in just thinking that you need someone to 'help out' without having a clear idea of what the job role will entail. Do you need someone full-time, part-time, temporary or permanent? What skills and qualifications do you need in your business? What soft skills are required to fulfil a new role? Remember – can you accommodate more staff? Will you need a larger office, a computer, desk or work station, phone, etc?

When you are clear on your requirements, you can create a detailed job description and person specification which will then allow you to create an attractive job advert. We'll look at these in more detail later on.

Replacing someone who is leaving your business

What if someone is leaving your employment? Do you really need to replace them? Ask yourself some simple questions first:

- Can the workload be shared out among other members of staff?
- Is there still a need for the tasks to be done?
- How can that job role change?
- Can that person be replaced by temporary or part-time staff?

These above points can only be resolved by you. I know there is a lot to think about, and we haven't even started yet. By knowing exactly why you want to take on a new employee, you have more focus to complete the recruiting and selection exercise.

So, you have identified a need for a new employee and have a clear idea of what tasks they are needed to do and the skills and experience that they need to have. Where do you go from here? You still need to gather more information.

Retention of good staff is more cost-effective than recruitment in terms of keeping knowledge, loyal service and customer relations. Exit interviews are an ideal way to find out why people are leaving your company. Are there any minor issues that can be resolved quickly? It may be that existing staff are just looking for a new challenge, more responsibility or different working hours. However, you might discover a deeper problem, such as the culture of the business, which will take some time to change. If there are more serious problems, these should be looked at as soon as possible, otherwise any new recruit will not last long and you will end up having to go through the whole recruitment and training process again, costing you time, money and productivity.

Ask other members of your staff to help identify what the department does and what else needs to be done by the new member of staff. This will also help to form the basis for the job description (JD) and person specification (PS). And it will help to give a better understanding of where the new employee will fit in to the company giving a larger picture.

It is always a good idea to check the local job market. See what jobs are in high demand and what other companies in your area are offering employees. Benchmark against your competitors by comparing your vacancy against similar vacancies will give you a good indication of advert wording and salary expectations. Local papers and internet recruitment sites are an excellent resource. The local Jobcentre can also provide information. National statistics will give an average pay for a specific job role in your area. This will give you an indication of whether you are paying too much or too little. Once you have all the information required, you can get to work on the recruitment process.

Creating a job description

Job descriptions are vital to the recruitment process. They provide information to the applicant and give you a structure to measure applicants against. Job descriptions must be as accurate as possible and should be updated as the role changes and develops. The key areas of a job description are:

- Job title
- Reporting lines
- Purpose of the role
- Main areas of responsibility
- General day-to-day duties
- Any other reasonable duties as requested

While the job title and reporting lines will be quite obvious, the other details will be provided through the information gathering exercise that you have already carried out.

The purpose of the role will explain why the role exists and how it fits into the organisation. The main areas of responsibility will give clear guidelines on what the role is expected to achieve. The general duties will set out the day-to-day tasks that are involved in the role and the standards of work that are expected. Always include the phase 'any other reasonable duties as requested'. This may seem unnecessary as it is expected that employees will follow instructions given by their manager, but this is not always the case. If I had £1 for every time I've worked with a client who has an employee who refuses to carry out additional duties and says "that's not my job", I would be a very rich woman today! You may need an employee to cover absences or holidays of staff in other departments. But remember, the additional tasks must be reasonable. Is it reasonable to ask an IT advisor to cover the reception desk for a week or two? Probably not. So additional tasks should be relevant to the employee's post.

Use the information you have gathered to complete a full job description. It should look something like Appendix 1.

Creating a person specification

Person specifications are often overlooked during the recruitment process, but they do provide a clear expectation of the skills and abilities that are needed for the post. The key areas of a person specification are:

- Experience and knowledge
- Qualifications
- Personal qualities and skills
- Key values

It is very important that you try to avoid any form of discrimination in a person specification. While you are outlining the personal aspects of your ideal employee, you must be mindful of equal opportunities. Try to avoid any wording that may be in protected characteristic under equality legislation, things like energetic, able bodied, young, etc.

The person specification will provide a standard to measure applicants against. It is unlikely that you will find the perfect candidate who will fit all your requirements.

Use the information you have gathered previously to complete a full person specification. It should look something like Appendix 2.

Advertising a vacancy

Now that you have your outline of the job role and the ideal candidate, you can proceed to advertising your vacancy. Your person specification should give a good indication of where you might be likely to find the ideal candidate from. This will help you to decide where to advertise. For example, if you are looking for a degree graduate with little experience required, you might want to contact local universities as they are always happy to pass on suitable vacancies to students. If on the other hand, you need someone with experience and fewer qualifications, you may find that internet and Jobcentre advertising work best.

There are a number of ways to advertise your vacancy. Here are just a few suggestions:

- Internet websites:
    - Company website
    - Gumtree
    - S1 Jobs
    - Indeed
    - Monster Jobs
    - LinkedIn
    - Facebook
    - Twitter
- Local papers
- Professional magazines
- Job centre
- Recruitment agencies
- Local schools, colleges and universities

I would normally suggest a mixed approach. Also bear in mind that local papers and recruitment agencies are expensive options, while some internet websites are free or cost very little. The placement of the advert should also reflect the level of post being recruited. I would not expect a higher management post to be advertised through the Jobcentre or on Gumtree, but a post at that level may be worth investing in a related job search website or magazine.

Word your advert very carefully. You don't want to give too much information, nor should it be too vague. You want potential candidates to be able to decide if they fit the post or not before they decide to apply. Give a brief outline of the role, the company and the benefits provided. Don't forget to include details of how to apply!

You must avoid all forms of potential discrimination in the advert. There should be no mention of age, gender, gender re-assignment, sexual orientation, marital status, physical or mental disability, pregnancy or parental status, race, nationality, country of origin, or religion. These are known as 'protected characteristics' under the Equality Act 2010, which we will look at later. There are some exceptions to this rule. For example, if you have a Chinese restaurant, then you can recruit for Asian employees only to maintain authenticity. If you are recruiting for a charity to support females who have been subject to physical abuse, then you can recruit for women-only employees. But always check current legislation to ensure you are not discriminating unlawfully in your recruitment process.

Here is an example of a suitable job advert:

JD Packing & Co.

Packing Assistant required to assist with all areas of packing and dispatch. Duties will include packing orders, dispatching orders, maintaining records and customer communication. Experience is preferred and training will be given. The post is full-time and is based at our warehouse in central Aberdeen.

Benefits include a competitive salary, pension and 30 days holiday per year.

Please make your application in writing with a full CV to Mr J Bloggs, 123 High Street, Aberdeen, AB10 5QR or email to j.blogs@jdpacking.co.uk. Closing date for all applications is Friday 18th November 2016.

CVs or Application forms

There is an age-old battle between the benefits of CVs versus Application forms. Let's have a look at what the benefits are.

Benefits of CVs:
- Cost-effective for the employer
- Most people have one prepared
- Can be sent electronically or by post

Benefits of Application forms:
- Standardised form to collect all information required
- Requires effort to complete (may reduce the likelihood of time wasters)

- Easy to find sections of interest – previous employment, qualifications, etc.
- Signed declaration of previous and current convictions
- Signed to show information given is correct

It is obvious that application forms offer the best benefits to the employer in terms of getting the correct information in a suitable format. However, there is the additional cost and time involved in printing and sending out application forms to potential employees. Technology can of course help out here. Most people are able to fill in an online application form and communication is much faster and easier with email. A downloadable application form on your company website may be the best option, but don't rule out CVs altogether.

Most job hunters will have a CV prepared and it can be a good initial indication of a candidate's suitability for a post. You may want to accept CVs initially and then ask the candidates to complete an application form in their words prior to interview. This may help to cut down on admin and costs while still ensuring you have the correct information in a suitable format and it is all signed off by the applicant.

Selection

It is important to consider how you will choose your applicants. What selection process will you follow? There are many selection methods, so it is vital that you have a plan on what selection methods you will use. Whichever methods you choose, you must be consistent with each applicant. It would be unfair to recruit for a post with a range of different selection methods and interview questions for each candidate. Have a structure in place for each recruitment project to ensure consistency and fairness. This will reduce the likelihood of any tribunal claims.

Here are a few selection methods that you can use. I recommend that you use a mix of these to give a broad view of each candidate:

- Telephone interview
- Face-to-face interview
- Interview score card
- Skills ability test
- Psychometric test
- Competency-based questioning
- Pressure testing

Telephone interview
This is often the first initial stage following the applications. It allows you to get the main information required and can help make a quicker decision on possible suitability of a candidate. It is particularly helpful if the job requires a lot of telephone communication.

Face-to-face interview
This is by far the most popular way of assessing candidates, not only to get to meet the candidate in person, but you can assess their personality and decide if they would be a good fit with the current team.

Interview score card
Use a score card to keep a record of the performance of each candidate during the interview and selection process. You can give a score for skills, experience, attitude, testing and even appearance. While some of the criteria are subjective, most of the criteria should be objective. Measure each candidate in the same way and have a guide for applying the score. The candidate with the highest score should be the best candidate. However, this may not always be the case. Sometimes, you just get a feel someone's suitability. Make sure you justify your

reasons for not recruiting the person with the highest score.

Skills ability test

This is a very useful selection method. The skills test must be suitable to the post being recruited for. It is not a work trial. The skills test must be set up in a suitable area and be assessed to meet criteria. It should only test the skills and experience that all candidates are expected to have. For example, a financial post may require a high level of Microsoft Excel skills. This can be tested by setting a task to be carried out within a set timescale. The test should last about 10-20 minutes. The results of the test can be reviewed during the interview with the candidate or after the interview with the interviewing panel.

Psychometric testing

There are mixed feelings about this method of selection, but if you do decide to use it, then make sure you are using a reputable psychometric testing method. Many companies use an external agent to conduct the test and provide professional feedback. It can give a good indication of aptitude and is usually most helpful in higher management positions.

Competency-based questioning

This is one of my personal favourite styles of interview. The questions should be set to allow the candidate to give examples of how they have dealt with certain situations or what they would do in a given scenario. This allows the candidate to talk you through their experiences and thought processes. It helps to give you an insight into how they prioritise things and what outcome they deem to be important. It can show where candidate may struggle with decision making, stress, deadlines and managing difficult situations. Of course, the questions still need to be relevant to the post.

Pressure testing
This interview style has its place if the post you are recruiting for has particular pressures. It is conducted like a 'good cop, bad cop' theme. The good cop should set the scenario and ask the candidate what they would do. Ask quick fire questions – 'what about this' or 'would you consider that'. Don't give the candidate much time to think things through. Continually ask if they are sure about their answers. This style does put pressure on the candidate and will make them question themselves. It may put some people off accepting the job if you make them an offer so use it wisely.

So now that you have your selection process mapped out and all the applications are in, you need to start your selection process. Your initial information gathering exercise will come in handy here again. As you sort through your applications, you want to match up the main criteria set out in the job description and person specification with the applications. Don't expect to have a handful of perfect candidates that tick all the boxes, but try to focus on the skills that are necessary for the role and be prepared to provide training on other skills. It is often the case that people management and organisations skills are talents that you either have or don't have. It can be very difficult to train someone on how to change their attitude. So if you are looking for a higher level post with responsibility for other members of staff, focus on their people skills. The finer details of the day-to-day job will be much easier to train in.

Split your application in to three sections: Yes, Maybe and No. If the Yes section is very small, then review the Maybe section again and pick out the best to add to the Yes section. However, if the initial Yes section has too many candidates, then review them again to weed out some of the weaker ones. Aim for about 3-6 Yes applicants to take forward.

Use the interview invitation letter (Appendix 3) to invite your top candidates to progress to the next stage of your selection process.

Interviewing skills

We have already identified a few different interview methods above. However, there are some key skills that will be helpful for interviewing candidates.

First and foremost, the interviewer must be confident and able to communicate clearly. It's a good idea to start the interview with an overview of the job duties and the skills required for the post. This will allow the candidate to direct their answers to fit your requirements. Therefore, it is helpful to have the department manager or supervisor present during the interview to help assess the candidates' suitability and technical knowledge.

Have a list of standard questions prepared. They must be relevant to the post you are recruiting for. Apply them consistently and take notes of answers given.

Avoid all areas of discrimination during interviews. We have already highlighted the main areas of discrimination, but you must avoid questions relating to gender, travel arrangements, family planning or childcare, disabilities, marital status, age or retirement plans, sexual orientation, race or religious beliefs, and all other personal life related issues.

Offer and rejections

Use the offer and rejection letters, (Appendices 4 and 5). The offer letter is normally sent out first, with the rejection letters being sent after the successful candidate has accepted. It would be quite embarrassing to go back to a rejected candidate and have to offer them the post.

Offer letters are legally binding so make sure you have the correct details on them. They should state the main key terms of employment that are being offered. You should always ask the new recruit to sign the letter to show their acceptance of the offer and return it to you as soon as possible. If there is some negotiation regarding the offer, an updated accurate offer should be sent.

Rejection letters should be short and sweet. Don't offer too much information as to why they have been unsuccessful, but you can allow them to contact you if they require feedback. Serious job hunters will want to know why they have been unsuccessful and how to improve going forward. Most candidates will not request feedback. Bear in mind that any feedback you give may be used at a tribunal if the unsuccessful candidate feels that they have been discriminated against. So be careful to avoid any areas of discrimination and stick to the score cards if possible. Candidates can see their own score card, but cannot see the score cards of the other applicants.

Of course, even an acceptance of an offer of employment in writing from the successful candidate does not guarantee that they will turn up for work on their first day. But bear in mind that the employment contract does not start until the new employee actually arrives on site. If for example, they phone in sick on their first day of work, they are not entitled to any sick pay as the employment has not legally started. But if they attend work then go home after a few minutes, they are entitled to sick pay because they have arrived on site and therefore the employment has legally begun.

Contracts of Employment

It is important to be aware of the written and psychological contracts and the differences between them.

The Written Contract

This is the basic contract which states the main terms and conditions of employment, which most people are familiar with. The contract is the bases of the employment agreement. It is an agreement between the employer and the employee which sets out the job role, hours and pay. Contracts of employment must be issued to each employee within 8 weeks of them starting employment with your company.

Before issuing a contract, refer to your earlier preparation information. Do you want to offer a part-time or full-time contract? Or maybe a zero hours contract? Will it be a permanent or temporary contract? If you decide to offer a permanent contract, do you want to have a set probationary period? Can you measure the employees' performance against some key performance indicators? There is a lot to think about to ensure you have the right contracts in place.

Whichever type of contract you issue, you must ensure it contains all the required information to comply with employment legislation. For example, the contract must contain the following information:

- name of employee
- name of employer
- job title
- job description overview
- hours of work
- place of work
- rate of pay
- holiday entitlements and calculations
- details of any collective agreements

It may also contain some additional information:

- sick pay entitlements
- pension scheme entitlements
- employee benefits
- disciplinary procedures
- grievance procedures

Bear in mind that written contracts may be sometimes be difficult to change in the future. If you want to grow and develop your business, then your contracts of employment must allow for a certain degree of flexibility.

It's also important to remember that all employees have the same employment rights. So a part-time contract will still offer the same protection in employment law as a full-time contract.

The Psychological Contract

This is a set of realistic expectations between the employer and the employee. The employer can expect the employee to turn up for work on time, dressed appropriately and provide a high level of customer service. The employee may expect the employer to provide training, recognition and give a certain degree of flexibility in working hours.

In order to achieve a balance between both types of contract, there are several areas which need to be addressed. At least some of these recommendations will need to be put in to practice as one in isolation will not be effective enough for you to see a real difference in a short space of time. These areas are:

- Communication and Involvement – business goals targets budgets
- Equality – diversity of staff, equal opportunities for training promotions

- People management – team-based environment, single absences
- Reward – incentives for good attendance, recognition for work
- Training and Development
- Culture – absence or work ethics

Induction

This is an area that is often overlooked in some companies. The induction is the ideal opportunity for your new member of staff to really get to know your business and understand the whole business culture.

Employment checks

It is a legal requirement that you check your new employee has the right to work in the UK from the first date of employment. This can be done in advance of the start date but must be after the offer of employment has been made to avoid any potential discrimination. If they don't have the right to work in the UK then you have to dismiss them based on a Statutory Requirement.

You must apply the check to every new member of staff, regardless of where you think they are from.

While a UK passport or National ID Card is the most common forms of acceptable ID, there is a list of alternatives available. In all cases, the original documents must be provided.

Acceptable ID documents include (list A documents):

- a current British passport,
- a National Identity Card (showing they are a member of the European Economic Area),
- a Residents' Permit or Workers' Registration Card,
- a Permanent Residence Card,
- a Biometric Immigration Document (showing indefinite UK residence),
- a Passport or travel document endorsement (showing exemption from immigration control),
- a Full British, Isle of Man Channel Islands or Irish Birth Certificate when presented with an official

document showing the National Insurance Number (P45 or NI Card),

- a Full British, Isle of Man Channel Islands or Irish Adoption Certificate when presented with an official document showing the National Insurance Number (P45 or NI Card),
- an official letter issued by the Home Office indicating the rights to work and live in the UK.

If none of the list A documents are available, then the following documents will be acceptable but will have to be re-checked annually to continue your statutory excuse (list B documents):

- a passport or travel document showing the person is allowed to do the type of work offered,
- a Biometric Immigration Document (showing allowance for the type of work offered),
- a work permit or similar showing allowance for the type of work offered (this must be shown with a passport or other travel document showing the right to be in the UK),
- a certificate of application to a family member of an EEA resident (this must have been issued within the 6 months previous to starting employment),
- an official letter issued by the Home Office indicating the allowance for the type of work offered (this must be shown with an official document showing the NI number).

When you receive the ID documents you are required to examine then carefully in order to:

- check that any photographs and birth dates on the documents match the appearance of the applicant
- check information in the job application against the documents produced to ensure the details match up

- satisfy yourself that the documents are valid, genuine, belong to the holder and have not been tampered with

With passports and travel documents, you must colour photocopy:

- the front cover
- all of the pages giving your potential employee's personal details including nationality
- any photographs and signatures
- the date of expiry
- pages containing a UK government stamp, or endorsement allowing your employee to do the work you are offering

Other documents including Workers' Registration Scheme cards will be copied in their entirety. This is to ensure the Company's Statutory Defence against illegal workers.

Copies of these documents must be signed by the recruiting manager or HR manager and kept in the employee's personnel file.

All copies made throughout the period for which the Company are employing the person must be retained for at least three years after they have left the company as recommended by HMRC.

These checks will identify which registration process, if any, the Company will be required follow. The Home Office's document checking service may be utilised from time to time if you feel unsure about anyone's rights to work in the UK.

Employee information

Of course there is other information that you will require in order to comply with various areas of legislation and best practice. I suggest the following information is taken from each new employee on the first day of employment during a welcome meeting:

- Current address and phone numbers
- Emergency contact details
- Bank details
- P45 from previous employment or benefits agency
- HMRC Starter Checklist if no P45 is available
- Current medical questionnaire and list of medications, if any

Bear in mind that all the information gathered is personal and sensitive and is therefore covered by the Data Protection Act. You must ensure you are not sharing this information with anyone other than those who need to know and that you are storing the information correctly, in a lockable filing cabinet for example.

Induction training

First day

Orientation is vital on the first day. Tell them all about your company and its values and objectives. Show around your premises and introduce them to key people that they will be working with. Don't forget to point out where the toilets and break facilities are located, along with any parking and lockers, etc.

A full health and safety induction is also vital and must be done as soon as possible, preferably on the first day.

As you know, written contracts are required by the eighth week of employment, but if you are well prepared, you can issue the contract on the first day too. I think it's best to get all the paperwork side of the induction over and done with as soon as possible, then you can focus on the rest of the induction and job role training. See Appendix 6 for an induction checklist that you can use in your company. It is important that the new employee signs it so you can prove that everything was covered, should there be any disputes later on.

First week
Training is a natural part of any induction process. You cannot expect any new member of staff to come in and automatically know your processes no matter how experienced they are in a particular role.

The first week should be all about getting to know the company and the people. Buddy the new start-up with someone different every day so they get to see the whole company in motion and not just the small area that they will be working on. This full company understanding will give the new employee a sense of what is required from them and why. Instead of cutting corners in their role, they will be able to appreciate the knock-on effect that their work has on other departments and is therefore much more likely to want to do a good job all round and will be more confident in communicating with other departments too. For example, if you are hiring a new finance administrator, let them spend some time working with purchasing to see how their processes work, and customer services to see what kind of issues come back from customers. And why not let them work with production so they have a good understanding of what your core business actually does.

Not only does a full induction process like this create a higher knowledge of the company, it also helps to create an emotional buy-in. This is what helps to drive the new employee forward and makes them want to do a good job for you. Think how you would feel having this kind of informative welcome to a new company compared to being sat in a corner and handed tasks to work on. You know it makes great business sense to invest a little extra time in your new start.

At the end of the first week, have a short meeting to discuss any queries that they might have. Address any issues that have arisen during the week and find out how the employee feels about the company as a whole. This is also a great time to shift the focus to how they will fit into the company in their new role and why it is so important.

First three months
When you are ready to start your new employee in their role, set some basic Key Performance Indicators (KPIs), maybe just two or three to start with. This can be anything from producing a report to updating a spreadsheet. Keep them simple and set a reasonable timescale. Review them at the end of the set time and set new KPIs for a longer time period, perhaps a month. Of course these ones will be a little more in depth and will therefore take a bit longer to complete.

Repeat this process, giving a little more responsibility and more challenging KPIs each time. Bear in mind that the whole point of having an induction is to introduce the new employee to the job, so don't expect them to be experts by the end of the first three months.

Have a formal review meeting with them after three months to assess their abilities, identify any training needs and to get feedback on how they think the role is progressing. It might be that they want to do more, or they might have some really good ideas on how to improve processes, so make sure this meeting involves two-way communication. A review meeting should never just be about you telling them what you think, it should be an open forum to discuss all aspects of the employment. If you are not the employee's direct supervisor, then invite the relevant supervisor to the meeting also. Take good notes during the meeting and summarise any key points at the end.

This is also a good opportunity to decide if you want to set further KPIs and a future review period. It is usual to have a three month and six month review as well as the normal annual performance reviews.

The records of review meetings can also be used should there be any conduct or capability issues that crop up in the future. For example, if a member of staff starts to show signs of persistent errors after a year of employment, you can refer to the early communications and training documents to demonstrate that these were discussed or that they never used to be a problem. Quite often, employees who perform poorly will try to blame the employer – "I wasn't trained on that" or 'you never said that was my job', etc. Life is much simpler in general if you keep good records with dates and signatures.

Communication & Involvement

For your employees to be involved in your business, *you* have to involve them. Open communications between all levels of staff. Think how your business operates communications at the moment. Is it on a need-to-know basis? Is communication from top to bottom, i.e. Management make decisions and inform lower levels of staff?

The ICE (Information and Consultation of Employees) Regulations 2004, currently affect organisations with 50 employees or more since April 2005. In a nutshell, this means that employees will have the right to know more information about the organisation that they are working for. Employers will be obligated to keep all members of staff informed about the business' economic activities, strategies, structure, employment and contractual relations. This can be done in a number of ways depending on the nature and size of the business. The recommended method for the standard provision is through the use of elected employee representatives. An agreement between the company and the elected employees should be in place to determine how and when the consultations will be held. To be valid the agreement must:

- be in writing
- cover all the employees in the undertaking
- set out how the employer will inform and consult employees or representatives
- be approved by employees

Minutes of each consultation meeting should be taken and made available for all staff.

Meetings
Sometimes it seems that there are just meetings about meetings and nothing really happens at any of them!

Management meetings are usually held on a regular basis and many different issues are discussed. This is a good time to highlight some information that can be passed on to all members of staff.

Mangers can then discuss this information with their department supervisors or team leaders who will, in turn, pass the information on to their teams of staff. It is important that all managers and team leaders are communicating the same information. This is a good method of organisational communication for organisations with less than 50 employees. Although it can be time consuming, it gives everyone a chance to raise any issues and ask questions about the information being shared. It is useful for building good relationships between shop floor staff and management. It helps to define the reporting lines through levels of management.

In smaller organisations, where are not so many levels of management to go through, it will improve communication and respect between management and staff. It also helps to make staff feel involved in the company and not just like a work donkey. It helps to maintain that initial buy-in that you worked so hard to create at the beginning of their employment.

Newsletters

Published weekly, bi-weekly or monthly to keep employees informed. This can combine a variety of information such as summary of meetings, targets achieved or set, introduce new members of staff, announce staff leaving and inform staff of any future events including training. You can also add an element of fun such as a company quiz or joke of the week.

It is a good idea to give all members of staff the opportunity to contribute to the newsletter. This will give them a sense of involvement and an added interest to the newsletter. They can contribute by offering an article or joke or become further involved by helping with the editing and distribution.

A few copies in the staff room will be enough for all to see. It does not need to be an expensive colour copy to every member of staff. If the technology is available, it could be sent out via email. But be careful not to exclude anyone from the list and make sure that all members of staff have access to it.

Notice Boards

These can be effective if they are kept up-to-date and well maintained. Notice boards should be placed in a prominent position where all staff have access to them. If your organisation is quite large, then several notice boards may be required. It is essential that they all contain the same information and are all updated at the same time so that no group of employees have access to information while others don't. Please be mindful of home working employees or those who work out with the main premises of the organisation, such as drivers.

Suggestion Boxes – involvement

Suggestion boxes give all employees the chance to put their view forward. Anonymous suggestions should always be an option as some people may not feel confident to speak out. Suggestions should be acknowledged and replied to as soon as possible – even if this is just a quick note to say that the suggested idea is being considered. It should be followed up with a full reply when possible.

Although this is an old method, it continues to work well in today's modern environment, as Vodafone discovered.

> *Vodafone is running a campaign to promote innovation in the workforce. "My big idea" has already generated 500 ideas from employees aimed at improving customer experience, products and services.*
>
> *The ideas amassed so far will be whittled down to five, with the finalists presenting their suggestions to the board later this month. The winning idea will be assessed for feasibility and rolled out next year.*
>
> *Dawn McIntyre, an HR business partner at Vodafone, told PM: "It's important to encourage staff to come up with ideas, and firms that don't do that are missing out as its key to employee satisfaction."*
>
> **Issue date:** *09 November 2006*
> **Source:** *People Management magazine*
> **Page:** *18*

Equality

In today's hugely diverse culture, it is more than likely that you will already have a diverse workforce. Employers have to accept that everyone is different in a range of ways. Equality is there to ensure that all members of staff and potential employees have equal opportunities in all areas of work.

The Equality Act was brought in to force in 2010 and incorporates 116 pieces of previous legislation under one single Act. It provides employers with a sound guide on how to promote equality at work and to be legally compliant with the current legislation.

The nine main pieces of legislation that have merged into the Equality Act are:

- the Equal Pay Act 1970
- the Sex Discrimination Act 1975
- the Race Relations Act 1976
- the Disability Discrimination Act 1995
- the Employment Equality (Religion or Belief) Regulations 2003
- the Employment Equality (Sexual Orientation) Regulations 2003
- the Employment Equality (Age) Regulations 2006
- the Equality Act 2006, Part 2
- the Equality Act (Sexual Orientation) Regulations 2007

The Act gives clear legal guidance on how employers should behave and how to manage certain situations, for example what to do when an employee develops a disability, or what process should be followed for an employee going though gender re-assignment.

The main thing to remember about equality at work is that everyone is there for the same reason, to do a good job for the company, and of course get paid for doing so! You should encourage your employees to treat everyone with respect and dignity all times. No one should feel discriminated against or bullied at work. Should you become aware of any such circumstances, you should put a stop to the negative behaviours immediately and make use of your company's disciplinary policy.

Conclusion

So, we've looked at all the key ingredients to recruiting the right staff, types of contracts of employment and how to conduct the perfect induction to welcome your new employee to your business. Follow this guidance and you can't go wrong.

But you know it doesn't just stop there, right? You can't just leave your staff to get on with it. There is still so much more you can do to make sure your staff feel happy and motivated at work. To make sure they stay with you for as long as possible and to make sure you get the best performance from them.

If you want your business to continue to grow and develop – and I'm sure you do – you want to manage your staff accordingly.

Keep any eye out for the rest of my books in the 'How-to HR' series which will look at how to ensure productivity and profit from your staff through key HR Management processes. To make sure you don't miss out, follow us on social media:

 https://www.facebook.com/SCRSolutionsLtd

 https://www.linkedin.com/in/jenimccabescrsolutions

 https://twitter.com/SCRSolutions

Appendices

Appendix 1 – Job Description

Job Description	
Job Title:	Packing Assistant
Department: **Reporting to:** **Responsible for:**	Dispatch Joe Blogs, Packing Manager No staff responsibilities
Purpose of the role	The main purpose of this role is to assist with the production of food products to fulfil orders and assist with the packaging in preparation for deliveries. The role will assist the company in providing neatly packaged products to customers within the set delivery timescales.
Main areas of responsibility	You will be responsible for ensuring you pack all products to the required standard to minimise damage during transportation. You must work to the required standards to maintain a well presented product.
General duties	**Your duties will consist of the following: -** **Food safety duties:** Maintain standards of cleanliness and hygiene in your working area at all times, Conduct quality control at key stages. **Communication:** Communicate effectively with customers in a professional manner, Answer customer queries via phone, email and face-to-face, Keep customers updated on the progress of their order delivery, Explain any problems and solutions in an

	understandable manner. **Administration:** Keep customer records up-to-date, Monitor and control stock levels, Ensure stock rotation, Complete customer orders to required specifications, Ensure all paperwork is completed and attached to the order for delivery, Liaise with other departments regarding deliveries – customer services, finance and production.
Any other reasonable duties as requested	You may be required to carry out other reasonable duties as requested. This may be due to a development within your role or as a temporary situation. All reasonable requests made by your manager must be complied with. Other duties may also include general housekeeping duties and Health and safety compliance.

Created by: Department Manager
Approved by: Director
Last updated: August 2015

Appendix 2 – Person Specification

Person Specification		
Job Title: Packing Assistant		
Department: Dispatch **Reporting to:** Joe Blogs, Packing Manager **Responsible for:** No staff responsibilities		
Experience & Knowledge	Essential: The post holder must be able to demonstrate an in depth knowledge of European packaging requirements. 2 years' experience is required in a similar environment.	Desirable: Previous experience of working in a food production company with stock and warehouse experience.
Qualifications	Essential: The post holder will have at least an SVQ level 2 or equivalent qualification in a warehouse related subject. A good standard of education is required including maths and English at National 4 or above.	Desirable: HNC or equivalent qualification in export.
Personal Qualities & Skills	Essential: The post holder must be able to communicate well on all levels. They will also have a high level of customer service skills. Attention to detail is required as is good organisational skills and the ability to priorities the workload.	Desirable: Fluent in English and one other European language.
Key Values	Essential: The post holder must be able to take pride in their work and will be accountable for any errors in orders sent to customers.	Desirable: A strong team player.
Created by: Department Manager **Approved by:** Director **Last updated:** August 2015		

Appendix 3 – Interview Invitation Letter

Emma Smith
123 Greenway Lane
GW1 2LA

5 August 2015

Dear Emma

Thank you for returning your completed application form and CV for the post of Packing Assistant.

I am pleased to invite you to an interview on 12th August at 2.30pm. The interview will be held at Packaging Company, 456 Boxway, BO4 6WY. Your interview will be held with Joe Blogs, Packaging Manager and Jane Tross, HR Manager.

On arrival, please report to the main reception and ask for Joe Blogs, Packaging Manager. During the interview, we will review your CV, ask competency-based questions and also carry out a skills test. The interview should last approximately 30 minutes.

Please confirm your attendance by phoning me on *01382 250333* and advise me if there are any specific requirements which you may have in relation to being able to attend the interview.

Yours sincerely,

Jane Tross
HR Manager

Appendix 4 – Employment Offer Letter

Emma Smith
123 Greenway Lane
GW1 2LA

15 August 2015

Dear Emma

I refer to your recent interview and am pleased to offer you the position of Packing Assistant.

Your hours of work will be (Insert weekly, monthly or annual hours) per week/month/year*. Your salary/wage* (Salary is paid monthly and wages are paid weekly. You can change this to an hourly rate of pay if you prefer.) will be £XX per hour/week/month*, payable at weekly/monthly* intervals by credit transfer to your nominated bank account. (Don't forget to delete the * options to suit.)

We would like you to start work on DATE, TIME (insert the start date and time. You may also want to add who they should report to on the first day).

This offer is subject to satisfactory references, your right to work in the UK and your acceptance of the standard terms set out in the Contract of Employment. A copy of the Contract will be supplied to you within 8 weeks of your start date.

Please bring your P45, bank details and your passport or National ID card with you on your first working day. (You can also add any additional information that you may require such as proof of qualifications or drivers licence, etc.)

If you have any questions about this offer please contact me as soon as possible on (Insert your phone number or email address). Otherwise, I would be grateful if you would confirm your acceptance of this offer by signing and returning one copy of this offer letter to me as soon as possible.

I look forward to hearing from you.

Yours sincerely,

Name
Title

I hereby accept the above offer:

Signed .... Dated ....

Appendix 5 – Employment Rejection Letter

Emma Smith
123 Greenway Lane
GW1 2LA

15 August 2015

Dear Emma

I refer to your recent interview and am sorry to inform you that you have not been successful in your application for the position of Packing Assistant.

If you require feedback on your interview, please do not hesitate to contact me on *01382 250333* or by email at j.blogs@packingcompany.co.uk.

I would like to thank you for your interest in the Company and wish you every success in finding future employment.

Yours sincerely,

Joe Blogs
Packing Manager

Appendix 6 – Induction Checklist

Induction Checklist

It is the responsibility of both management and new start employee to ensure that all relevant items are properly covered during the induction period. Please return the completed form to the Human Resources Department.

Name .... Start Date ....

Job Title .... Department ....

Payroll number ....

Introduction to the company	Completed by:	Comments:
• Mission Statement • Who's who - Buddy • History of Company • Products/services/markets • Future plans and developments		
Terms and conditions of employment • Written terms and conditions issued • Hours, breaks, method of payment • Holidays • Clocking on/flexitime/reporting procedures • Probationary / Temporary period • Period of notice • Sickness provisions • Pension provisions		

IT	Completed by:	Comments:
<ul><li>Computer log-in details</li><li>Security</li><li>Hardware received</li></ul>		
Health and safety <ul><li>Awareness of hazards – any particular to type of work</li><li>Safety rules</li><li>Emergency procedures</li><li>Clear gangways, exits</li><li>Location of exits</li><li>Dangerous substances or processes</li><li>Reporting of accidents</li><li>First aid</li><li>Personal hygiene</li><li>Introduction to safety representative</li></ul>		
Equal opportunities policy and worker development <ul><li>Training provision</li><li>Further education/training policies</li><li>Performance appraisal</li><li>Promotion avenues</li></ul>		
Worker/employer relations <ul><li>Trade union membership</li><li>Other worker representation</li><li>Worker communications and consultation</li><li>Grievance and disciplinary procedure</li><li>Appeals procedure</li></ul>		

Organisation rules	Completed by:	Comments:
<ul><li>Smoking policy</li><li>General behaviour/dress code</li><li>Telephone calls</li><li>Canteen/break facilities</li><li>Cloakroom/toilets/lockers</li></ul>		
Welfare and worker benefits / facilities<ul><li>Protective clothing – supply, laundry, replacement</li><li>Medical services</li><li>Parking arrangements</li><li>Company discounts</li></ul>		

If you have any further queries regarding your induction and employment at *Packing Company*, please contact your immediate supervisor or human resources.

I have received a full induction as indicated above and I agree to abide by the standards set out by *Packing Company*.

Signed .... Dated ....

www.ingramcontent.com/pod-product-compliance
Lightning Source LLC
Chambersburg PA
CBHW071831200526
45169CB00018B/1328